CAMPFIRE SONGS FOR BANJO

T0088364

ISBN 978-1-5400-4675-8

Visit Hal Leonard Online at
www.halleonard.com

Contact us:
Hal Leonard
7777 West Bluemound Road
Milwaukee, WI 53213
Email: info@halleonard.com

In Europe, contact:
Hal Leonard Europe Limited
42 Wigmore Street
Marylebone, London, W1U 2RN
Email: info@halleonardeurope.com

In Australia, contact:
Hal Leonard Australia Pty. Ltd.
4 Lentara Court
Cheltenham, Victoria, 3192 Australia
Email: info@halleonard.com.au

Amie

Words and Music by Craig Fuller

keep you for ____ my own. _____

Chorus

A - mie,

what you wan - na do? _____ I think

I could stay with you ____ for a while, ___ may - be long -

To Coda **Interlude**

- er if I do. _____

|1., 2. |3.   *D.C. al Coda*

Additional Lyrics

2. Don't you think the time is right for us to find
   All the things we thought weren't proper
   Could be right in time, and can you see
   Which way we should turn together or alone?
   I can never see what's right or what is wrong.
   Would it take too long to see?

4. Now it's come to what you want; you've had your way.
   And all the things you thought before
   Just faded into gray, and can you see
   That I don't know if it's you or if it's me?
   If it's one of us, I'm sure we both will see.
   Won't ya look at me and tell me...

Blowin' in the Wind

Words and Music by Bob Dylan

1. How man-y roads ___ must a man ___ walk _ down _
2., 3. *See additional lyrics*

be - fore ___ you call ___ him a man? ___

How man-y seas ___ must a white ___ dove _ sail _

be - fore ___ she sleeps in the sand? ___

Yes, and how ___ man-y times ___ must the can -

non - balls __ fly _____ be - fore _____ they are for -

- ev - er banned? __ The an -

Chorus

- swer, my friend, ____ is blow - in' in ____ the wind. __

_____ The an - swer is blow - in' in _____ the wind. __

1., 2. | 3.

Additional Lyrics

2. How many years can a mountain exist
   Before it is washed to the sea?
   How many years can some people exist
   Before they're allowed to be free?
   Yes, and how many times can a man turn his head
   And pretend that he just doesn't see?

3. How many times must a man look up
   Before he can see the sky?
   How many ears must one man have
   Before he can hear people cry?
   Yes, and how many deaths will it take till he knows
   That too many people have died?

Brown Eyed Girl

Words and Music by Van Morrison

First note

Verse
Moderately fast Rock

1. Hey, where did we ____ go   days when the rains ___
2., 3. *See additional lyrics*

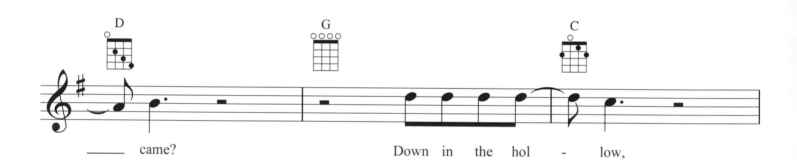

____ came?   Down in the hol - low,

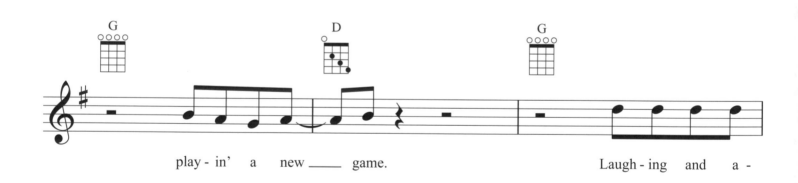

play - in' a new ____ game.   Laugh - ing and a -

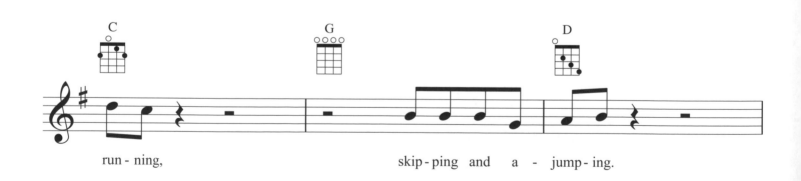

run - ning,   skip - ping and a - jump - ing.

in the mist - y morn - ing fog ___ with   our

hearts a - thump - in', and you, _____   my brown eyed girl. ___

___   You, _____

1.

_____   my brown eyed   girl. _____

2.

Do you re - mem - ber when ___   we used to sing: ___

Chorus

___ Sha, la, ___ la, la, ___ la, la, ___ la, la, ___ la, la, la, te, da? ___

Sha, la, ___ la, la, ___ la, la, ___ la, la, ___ la, la, la, te, da. ___

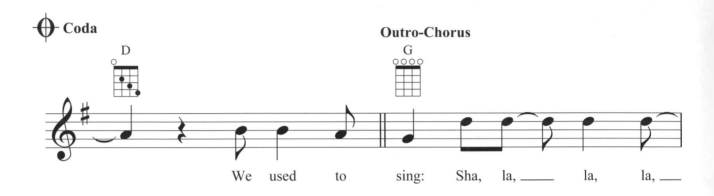

We used to sing: Sha, la, ___ la, la, ___

___ la, la, ___ la, la, ___ la, la, la, te, da. ___ Brown eyed girl.

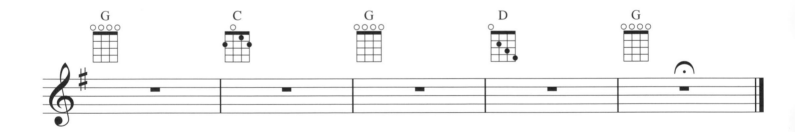

Additional Lyrics

2. Whatever happened
   To Tuesday and so slow?
   Going down the old mine
   With a transistor radio.
   Standing in the sunlight laughing,
   Hiding behind a rainbow's wall,
   Slipping and sliding
   All along the waterfall with you,
   My brown eyed girl.
   You, my brown eyed girl.

3. So hard to find my way
   Now that I'm all on my own.
   I saw you just the other day;
   My, how you have grown.
   Cast my mem'ry back there, Lord.
   Sometimes I'm overcome thinking 'bout it.
   Laughing and a-running, hey, hey,
   Behind the stadium with you,
   My brown eyed girl.
   You, my brown eyed girl.

Don't Worry, Be Happy

Words and Music by Bobby McFerrin

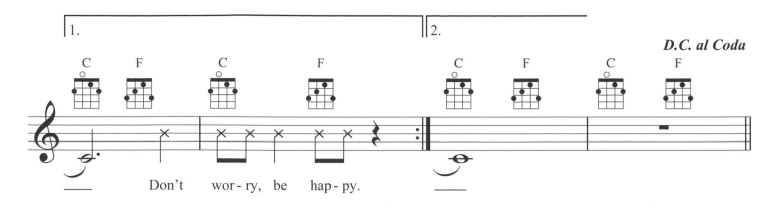

D.C. al Coda

Don't wor-ry, be hap-py.

Coda

Outro-Chorus

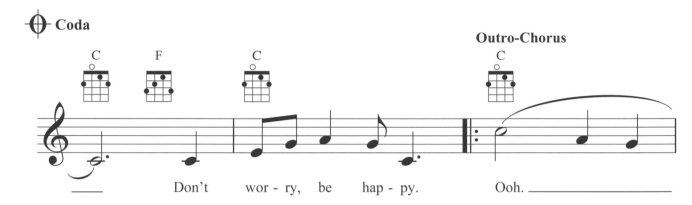

Don't wor-ry, be hap-py. Ooh. _____

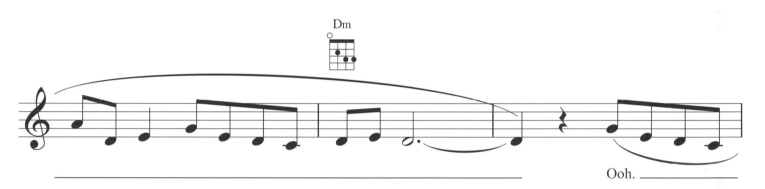

Ooh. _____

Repeat and fade

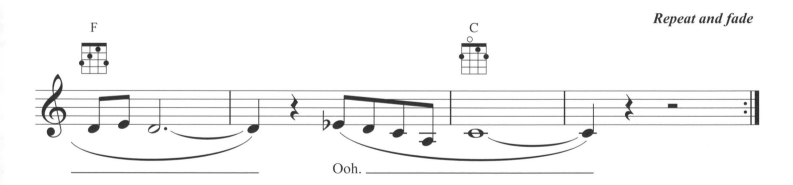

Ooh. _____

Additional Lyrics

2. Ain't got no place to lay your head.
   Somebody came and took your bed.
   Don't worry, be happy.
   The landlord say your rent is late,
   He may have to litigate.
   Don't worry, be happy.
   (Spoken:) Look at me—I'm happy.

3. Ain't got no cash, ain't got no style.
   Ain't got no gal to make you smile.
   Don't worry, be happy.
   'Cause when you worry your face will frown,
   And that will bring ev'rybody down.
   Don't worry, be happy.
   Don't worry, be happy now.

The Campfire Song Song

Words and Music by Carl Williams, Dan Povenmire, Jay Lender, Michael Culross and Michael Walker

*Let chord ring.

Chorus (faster each time)

C-A-M-P - F-I-R-E S-O-N-G song.

C-A-M-P - F-I-R-E S-O-N-G song. And if

you don't think that we can sing it fast - er, then you're

1.

wrong. But it - 'll help if you just sing a - long. _____

2. **Outro** **Slower**

wrong. It - 'll help, _____ it - 'll help _____ if you just sing a -

long.

Edelweiss

Lyrics by Oscar Hammerstein II
Music by Richard Rodgers

Bridge

Blos - som of snow, may you bloom and

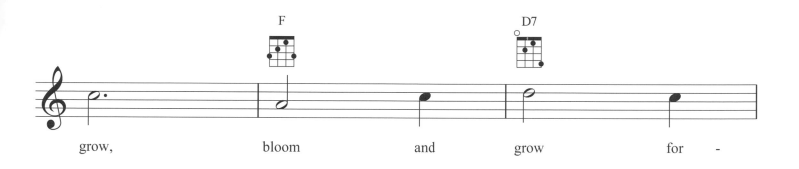

grow, bloom and grow for -

Chorus

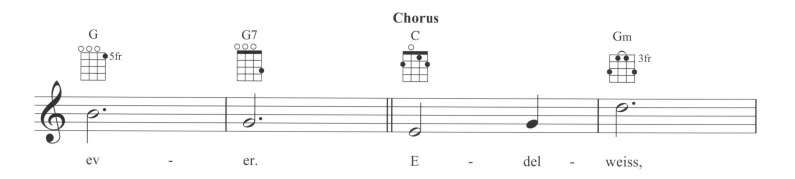

ev - er. E - del - weiss,

e - del - weiss, bless my

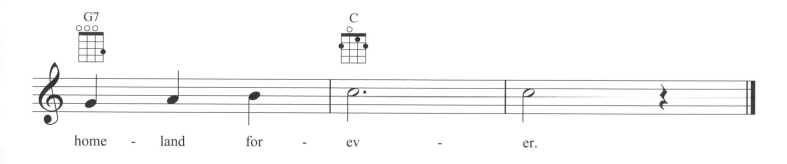

home - land for - ev - er.

Folsom Prison Blues

Words and Music by John R. Cash

First note

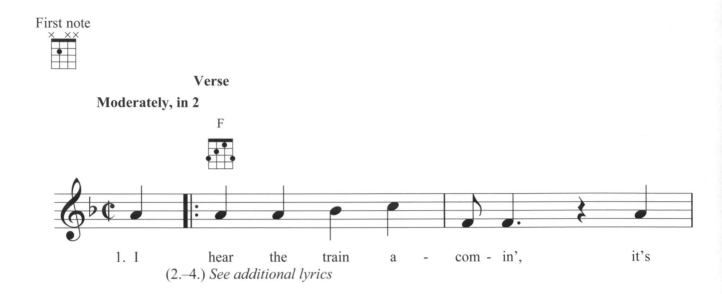

Verse

Moderately, in 2

1. I hear the train a - com - in', it's

(2.–4.) *See additional lyrics*

roll - in' 'round the bend, ____ and I ain't seen the sun -

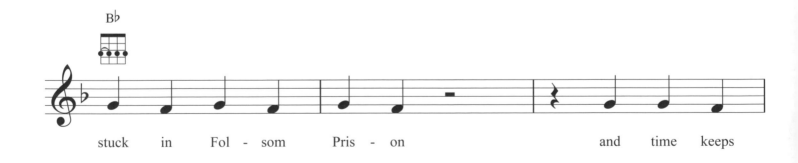

- shine since I don't ____ know when. I'm

stuck in Fol - som Pris - on and time keeps

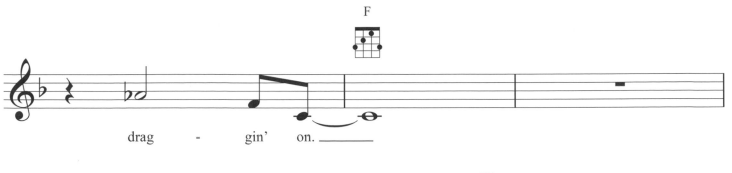

drag - gin' on. _____

But that train keeps a roll -

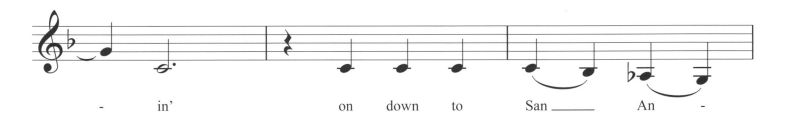

- in' on down to San _____ An -

tone.

2. When
3. I
4. Well, if they

Additional Lyrics

2. When I was just a baby, my mama told me, "Son,
   Always be a good boy; don't ever play with guns."
   But I shot a man in Reno, just to watch him die.
   When I hear that whistle blowin', I hang my head and cry.

3. I bet there's rich folks eatin' in a fancy dining car.
   They're prob'ly drinkin' coffee and smokin' big cigars.
   Well, I know I had it comin', I know I can't be free.
   But those people keep a-movin' and that's what tortures me.

4. Well, if they freed me from this prison, if that railroad train was mine,
   I bet I'd move it on a little farther down the line.
   Far from Folsom Prison, that's where I want to stay,
   And I'd let that lonesome whistle blow my blues away.

The Gambler

Words and Music by Don Schlitz

and he be-gan to speak. 2. He said, right." You got to
3. So, I keep.
5. So, ___

Chorus

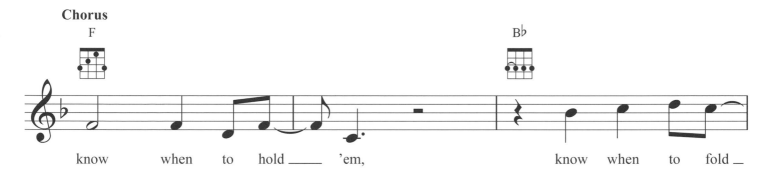

know when to hold ___ 'em, know when to fold ___

___ 'em, know when to walk ___ a - way, ___

and know when to run. ___ You nev - er count your

mon - ey when you're sit - tin' at the ta -

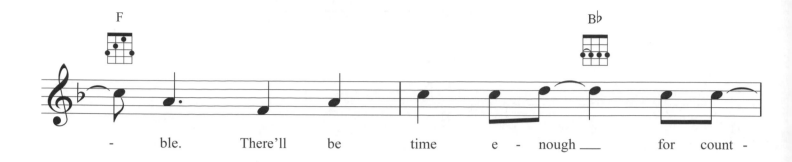

- ble. There'll be time e - nough ___ for count -

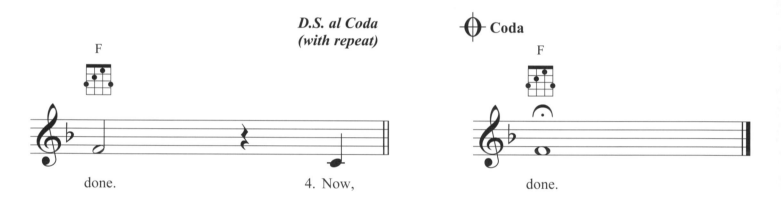

To Coda ⊕

- in' when the deal - in's

D.S. al Coda
(with repeat)

⊕ **Coda**

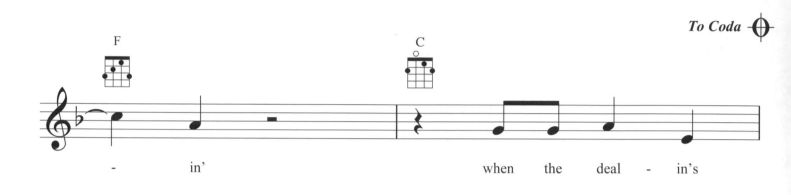

done. 4. Now, done.

Additional Lyrics

2. He said, "Son, I've made my life out of readin' people's faces,
And knowin' what their cards were by the way they held their eyes.
So if you don't mind me sayin', I can see you're out of aces.
For a taste of your whiskey, I'll give you some advice."

3. So, I handed him my bottle and he drank down my last swallow.
Then he bummed a cigarette and asked me for a light.
And the night got deathly quiet, and his face lost all expression,
Said, "If you're gonna play the game, boy, you gotta learn to play it right."

4. Now, ev'ry gambler knows the secret to survivin'
Is knowing what to throw away and knowin' what to keep.
'Cause ev'ry hand's a winner and ev'ry hand's a loser,
And the best you can hope for is to die in your sleep.

5. So, when he'd finished speakin', he turned back toward the window,
Crushed out his cigarette and faded off to sleep.
Then somewhere in the darkness, the gambler, he broke even,
But in his final words I found an ace that I could keep.

Drift Away

Words and Music by Mentor Williams

Oh, give me the beat, boys, and free my soul. I wan - na get lost in your rock and roll and drift a - way.

Oh, give me the beat, boys, and free my soul. I wan - na get lost in your rock and roll and drift a - way.

To Coda

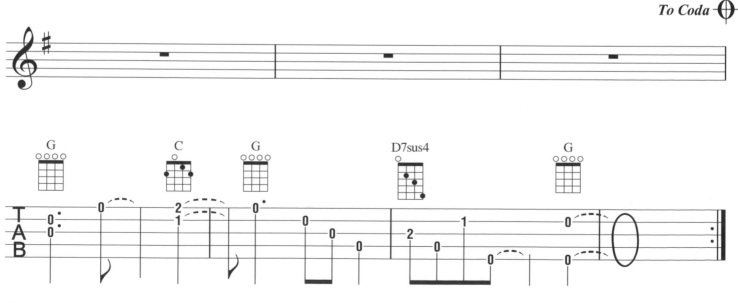

Bridge

And when my mind _____ is free, _____

you know a mel - o - dy can move _____ me.

And when I'm feel - in' blue, _____

the gui - tar's com - in' through _ to

D.C. al Coda   ⊕ **Coda**

soothe me. _____

Additional Lyrics

2. Beginnin' to think that I'm wastin' time.
   I don't understand the things I do.
   The world outside looks so unkind,
   And I'm countin' on you to carry me through.

3. Thanks for the joy that you've given me.
   I want you to know I believe in your song
   And rhythm and rhyme and harmony.
   You help me along, makin' me strong.

Hallelujah

Words and Music by Leonard Cohen

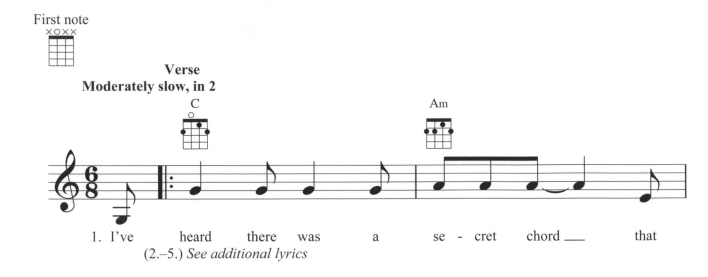

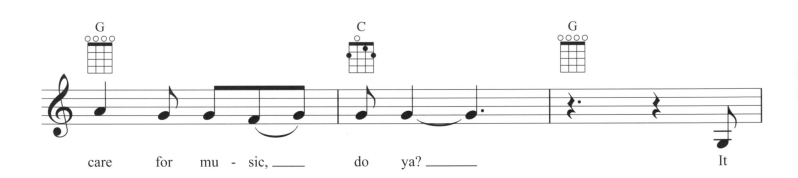

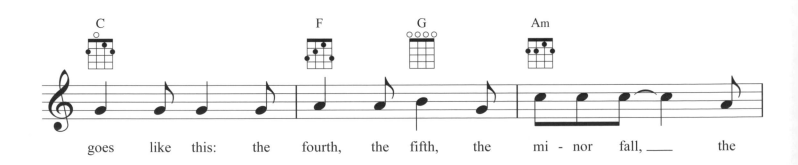

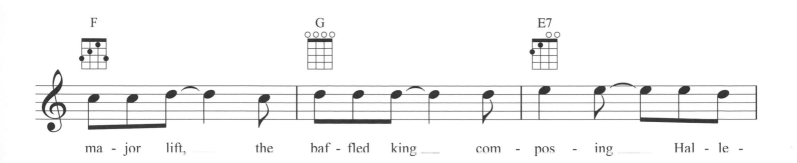

ma - jor lift, ____ the baf - fled king ___ com - pos - ing ____ Hal - le -

Chorus

lu - jah. _____ Hal - le - lu - jah, _____ hal - le -

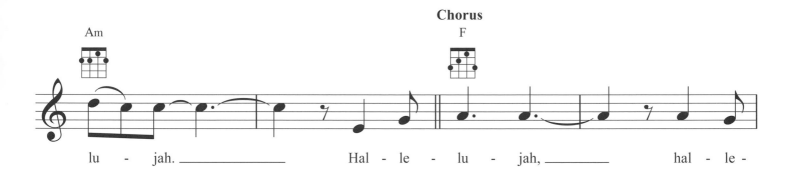

lu - jah, _____ hal - le - lu - jah, _____ hal - le -

1.–4.

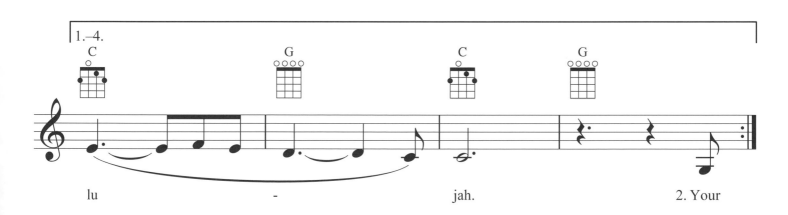

lu - jah. 2. Your

5.

Outro-Chorus

lu - jah. Hal - le - lu - jah. _____ Hal - le -

lu - jah. _____ Hal - le - lu - jah. _____ Hal - le -

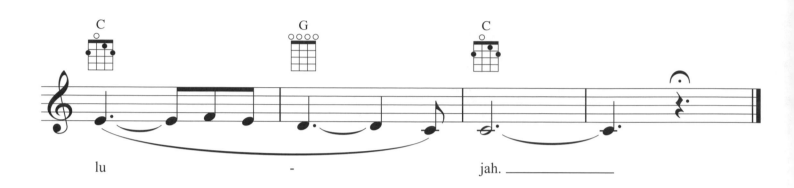

lu - jah. _____

Additional Lyrics

2. Your faith was strong but you needed proof.
   You saw her bathing on the roof.
   Her beauty and the moonlight overthrew ya.
   She tied you to a kitchen chair.
   She broke your throne, she cut your hair.
   And from your lips she drew the Hallelujah.

3. Maybe I have been here before.
   I know this room, I've walked this floor.
   I used to live alone before I knew ya.
   I've seen your flag on the marble arch.
   Love is not a vict'ry march.
   It's a cold and it's a broken Hallelujah.

4. There was a time you let me know
   What's real and going on below.
   But now you never show it to me, do ya?
   And remember when I moved in you.
   The holy dove was movin', too,
   And every breath we drew was Hallelujah.

5. Maybe there's a God above,
   And all I ever learned from love
   Was how to shoot at someone who outdrew ya.
   And it's not a cry you can hear at night.
   It's not somebody who's seen the light.
   It's a cold and it's a broken Hallelujah.

God Bless the U.S.A.

Words and Music by Lee Greenwood

won't for-get the men who died, __ who gave that right to me. And I'll glad-ly

stand up next to you _____ and de-fend her still to-day, 'cause there

To Coda ⊕

ain't no doubt I love this land. _____ God bless the U. S. A.

Verse

2. From the lakes of Min-ne-so-ta _____ to the hills of Ten-nes-see, ____ a-

cross the plains of Tex-as, from sea to shin-ing sea, ____ from

De-troit down to Hous-ton and New York to L. A., well, there's

pride in ev-'ry A-mer-i-can heart, and it's time to stand and say _____ that I'm

Coda

Outro-Chorus

A. _____ And I'm proud to be an A-mer-i-can ___ where at

least I know I'm free. And I won't for-get the men who died, ___ who

gave that right to me. And I'll glad-ly stand up next to you ___ and de-

fend her still to-day, 'cause there ain't no doubt I love this land. ___

_____ God bless the U. S. A.

Hello Mudduh, Hello Fadduh!

(A Letter from Camp)

Words by Allan Sherman
Music by Lou Busch

i - vy. You re - mem - ber Leo - nard Skin - ner? He got
lar - ia. You re - mem - ber Jef - frey Har - dy? They're a -

pto - maine poi - s'ning last night af - ter din - ner. 2. All the
bout to or - gan - ize a search - ing par - ty.

Bridge

Take me home, oh, Mud - duh, Fad - duh, take me
Take me home, I prom - ise I will not make

home, I hate Gra - na - da. Don't leave me out in the for - est
noise, or mess the house with oth - er boys. Oh, please don't make me

where I might get eat - en by a bear.

stay; I've been here one whole day! 3. Dear - est

Verse

Fad - duh, dar - ling Mud - duh, how's my pre - cious lit - tle

brud - duh? Let me come home if you miss me. I would

e - ven let Aunt Ber - tha hug and kiss me. Wait a

min - ute; it stopped hail - ing. Guys are swim - ming, guys are

sail - ing! Play - ing base - ball, gee, that's bet - ter. Mud - duh,

Fad - duh, kind - ly dis - re - gard this let - ter.

Leaving on a Jet Plane

Words and Music by John Denver

blow - in' his horn. __ Al - read - y I'm so lone - some I could
sing for you. __ When I come back I'll bring your wed - ding
leave a - lone, __ a - bout the times I won't have to

Chorus

die. _____ So kiss
ring. _____ So kiss } me and smile for me, ____
say: _____ Kiss }

tell me that ____ you'll wait for me, ____ hold me like ____ you'll

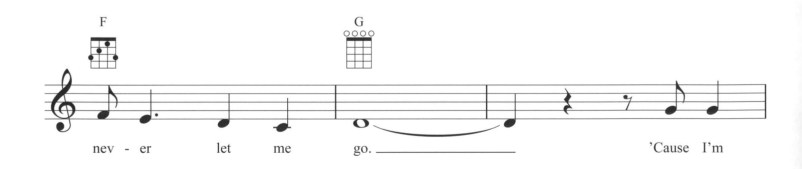

nev - er let me go. _____ 'Cause I'm

leav - in' on a jet ____ plane, don't know when

I'll be back ___ a - gain. ___ Oh, babe, I hate to

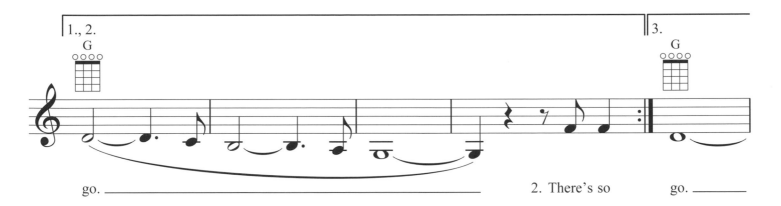

1., 2.

go. ___ 2. There's so

3.

go. ___

Outro

___ I'm leav - in' on a jet ___ plane, don't know when

I'll be back ___ a - gain. ___ Oh, babe, ___ I hate to

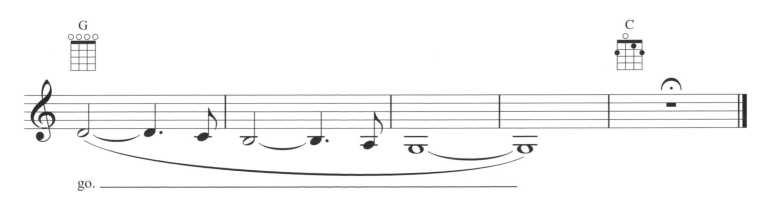

go. ___

The House of the Rising Sun

Words and Music by Alan Price

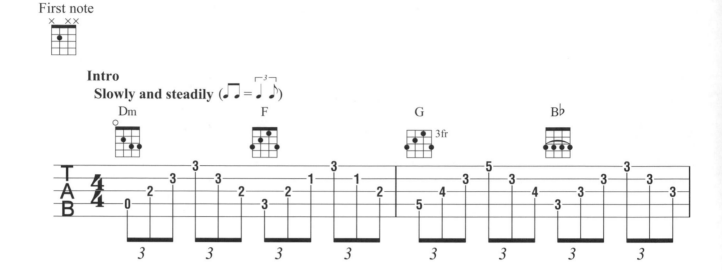

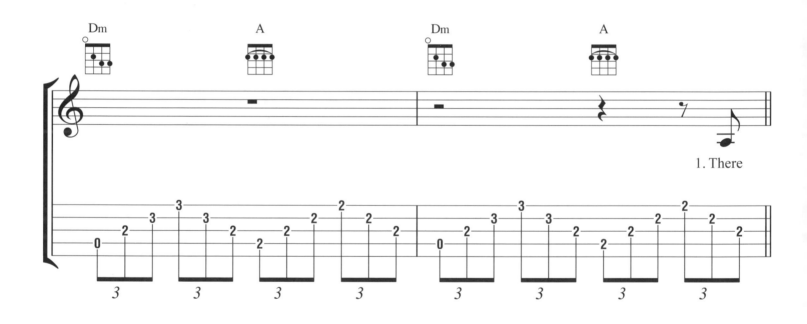

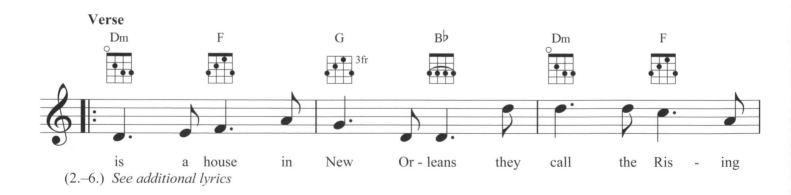

(2.–6.) *See additional lyrics*

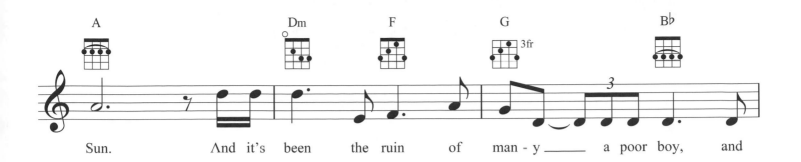

Sun. And it's been the ruin of man-y _____ a poor boy, and

God, I know _____ I'm one.

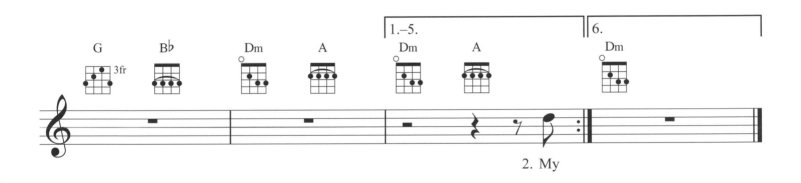

2. My

Additional Lyrics

2. My mother was a tailor, sewed my new blue jeans.
   My father was a gamblin' man down in New Orleans.

3. Now, the only thing a gambler needs is a suitcase and a trunk.
   And the only time he'll be satisfied is when he's on a drunk.

4. Oh! mother, tell your children not to do what I have done:
   Spend your lives in sin and misery in the House of the Rising Sun.

5. Well, I've got one foot on the platform, the other foot on the train.
   I'm going back to New Orleans to wear that ball and chain.

6. Well, there is a house in New Orleans they call the Rising Sun.
   And it's been the ruin of many a poor boy, and God, I know I'm one.

I Walk the Line

Words and Music by John R. Cash

First note

Verse

Moderately bright, in 2

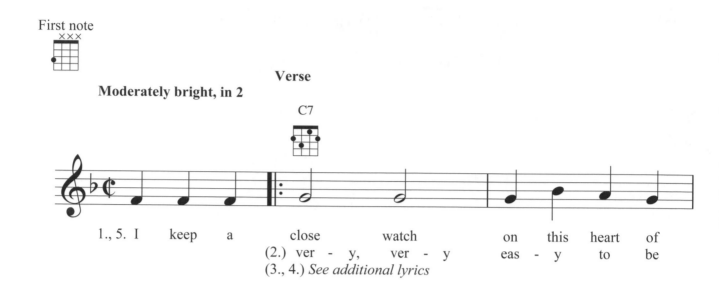

1., 5. I keep a close watch on this heart of
(2.) ver - y, ver - y eas - y to be
(3., 4.) *See additional lyrics*

mine. _____ I keep my eyes wide
true. _____ I find my - self a - lone

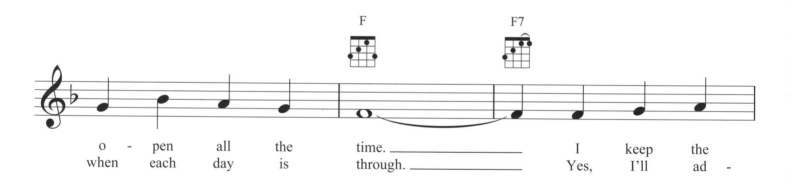

o - pen all the time. _____ I keep the
when each day is through. _____ Yes, I'll ad -

ends out for the tie that binds. _____
mit that I'm a fool for you. _____

C7

Be - cause you're mine, _____

1., 2.
F

_____ I walk the line. _____

3.
F

_____ 2. I find it line. _____
3. As sure as
4. You've got a

Additional Lyrics

2. As sure as night is dark and day is light,
I keep you on my mind both day and night.
And happiness I've known proves that it's right.
Because you're mine, I walk the line.

3. You've got a way to keep me on your side.
You give me a cause for love that I can't hide.
For you I know I'd even try to turn the tide.
Because you're mine, I walk the line.

I'd Like to Teach the World to Sing

Words and Music by Bill Backer, Roquel Davis, Roger Cook and Roger Greenaway

First note

Verse

Happily

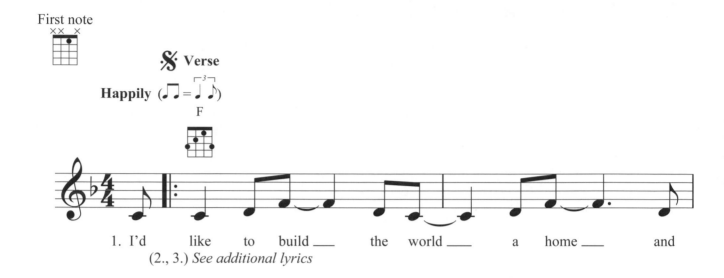

1. I'd like to build ___ the world ___ a home ___ and

(2., 3.) *See additional lyrics*

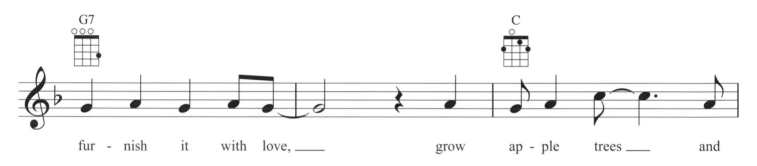

fur - nish it with love, ___ grow ap - ple trees ___ and

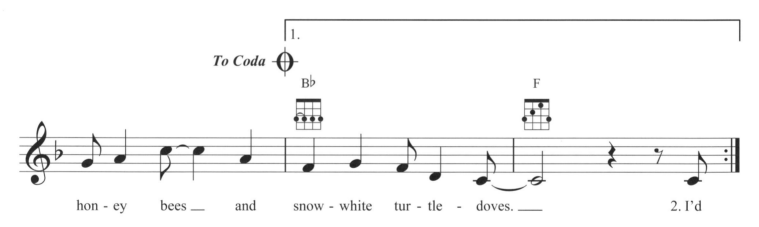

To Coda

1.

hon - ey bees ___ and snow - white tur - tle - doves. ___ 2. I'd

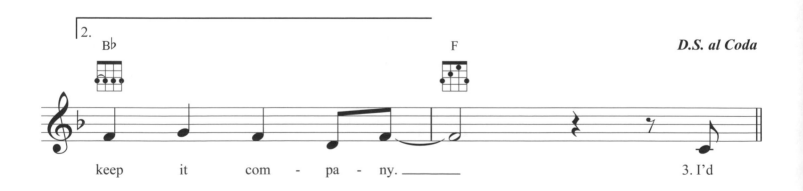

2.

D.S. al Coda

keep it com - pa - ny. ___ 3. I'd

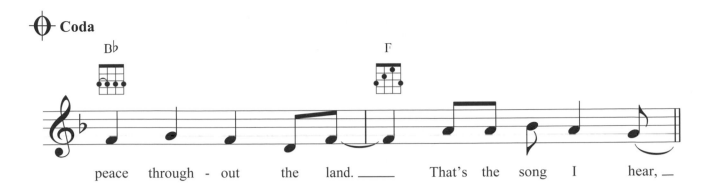

Coda

peace through - out the land. _____ That's the song I hear, __

Bridge

___ let the world sing to - day.

Outro

I'd like to teach ___ the world ___ to sing ___ in

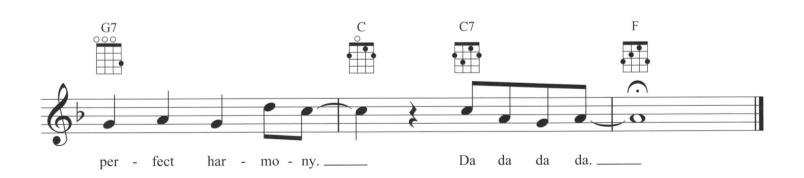

per - fect har - mo - ny. _____ Da da da da. _____

Additional Lyrics

2. I'd like to teach the world to sing in perfect harmony.
   I'd like to hold it in my arms and keep it company.

3. I'd like to see the world, for once, all standing hand in hand,
   And hear them echo through the hills for peace throughout the land.

Lean on Me

Words and Music by Bill Withers

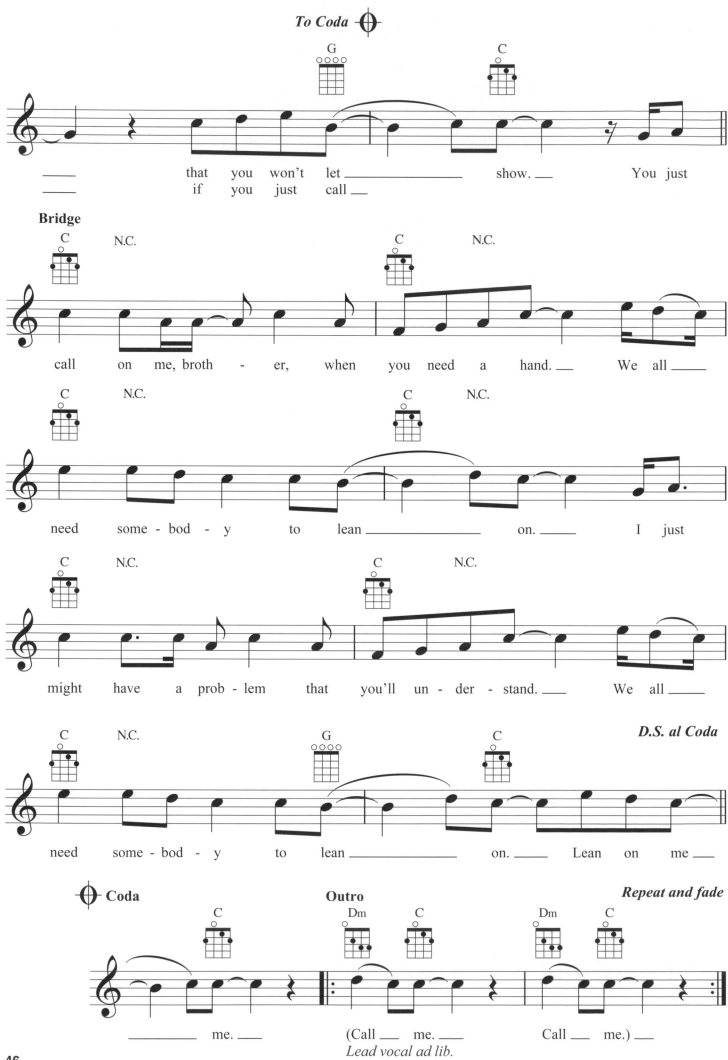

Let It Be

Words and Music by John Lennon and Paul McCartney

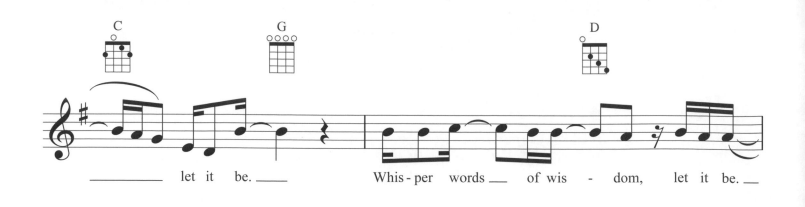

_____ let it be. ____ Whis - per words ___ of wis - dom, let it be. __

Verse

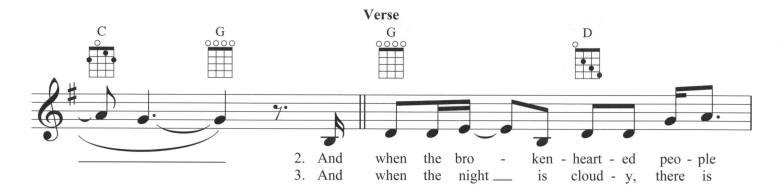

_____ 2. And when the bro - ken - heart - ed peo - ple
3. And when the night ___ is cloud - y, there is

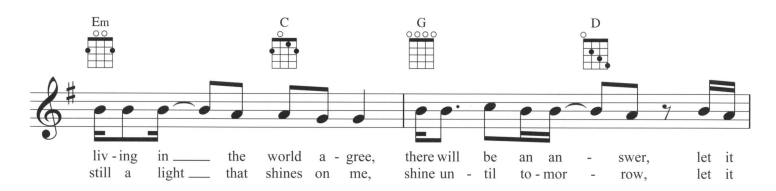

liv - ing in ____ the world a - gree, there will be an an - swer, let it
still a light ___ that shines on me, shine un - til to - mor - row, let it

be. _____ For though they may be part - ed, there is
be. _____ I wake up to the sound ___ of mu - sic,

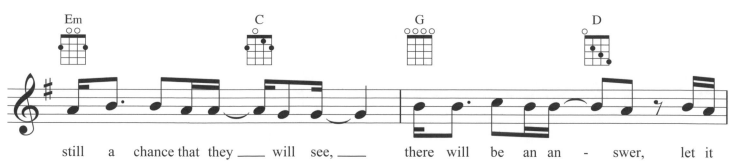

still a chance that they ___ will see, ___ there will be an an - swer, let it
Moth - er Mar - y comes ___ to me, ___ speak - ing words of wis - dom, let it

Mountain Dew

Words and Music by Scott Wiseman and Bascomb Lunsford

On Top of Spaghetti

Words and Music by Tom Glazer

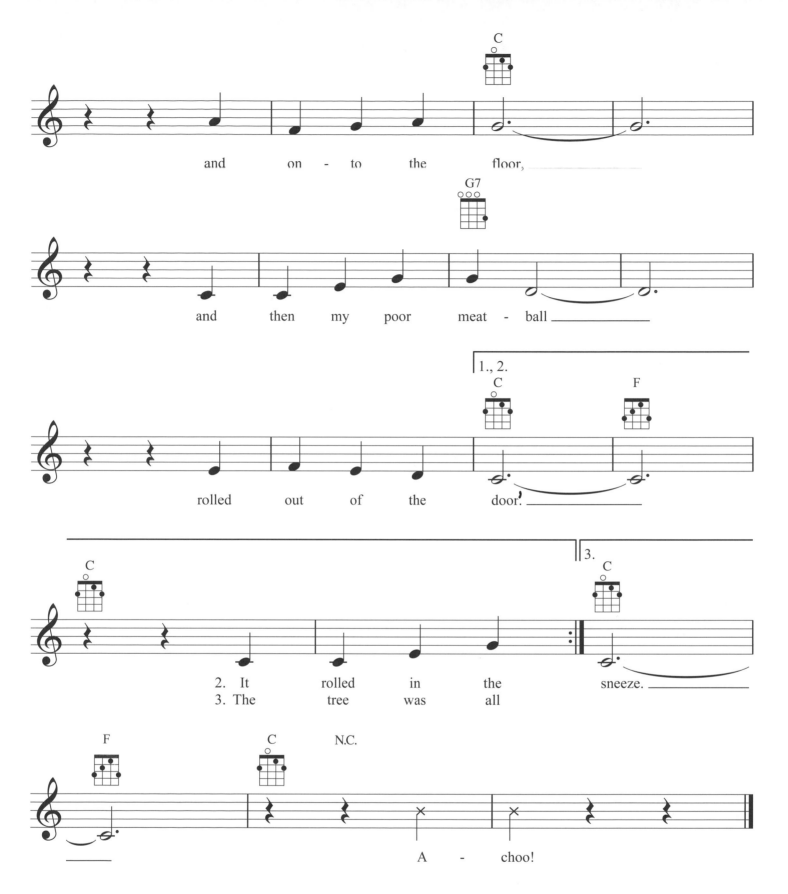

Additional Lyrics

2. It rolled in the garden and under a bush,
   And then my poor meatball was nothing but mush.
   The mush was as tasty as tasty could be,
   And early next summer, it grew into a tree.

3. The tree was all covered with beautiful moss;
   It grew lovely meatballs and tomato sauce.
   So if you eat spaghetti all covered with cheese,
   Hold onto your meatballs and don't ever sneeze.

Peaceful Easy Feeling

Words and Music by Jack Tempchin

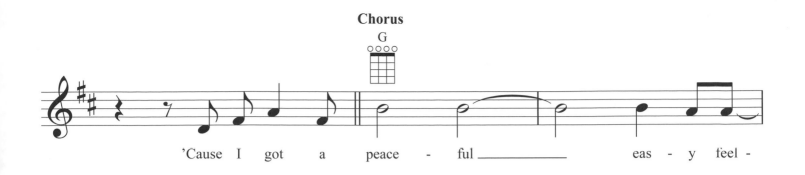

Chorus

'Cause I got a peace - ful _____ eas - y feel -

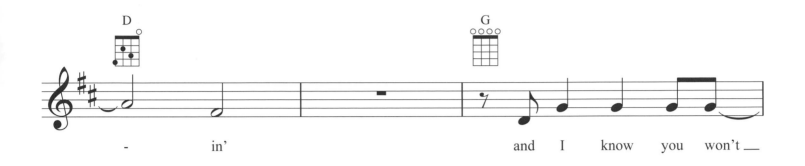

- in' and I know you won't __

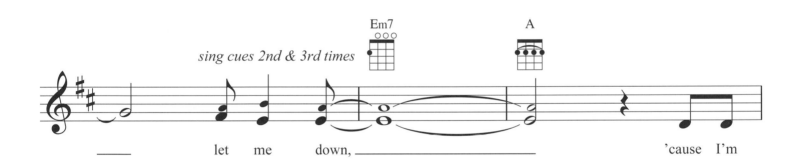

sing cues 2nd & 3rd times

__ let me down, _____ 'cause I'm

To Coda

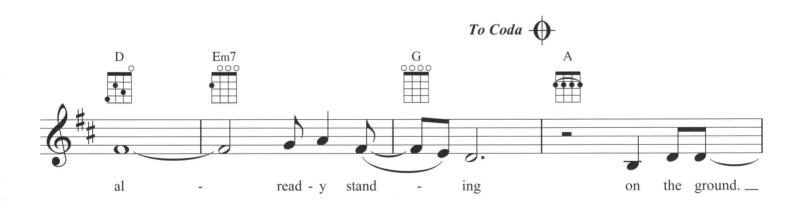

al - read - y stand - ing on the ground. __

2nd time, D.C. al Coda

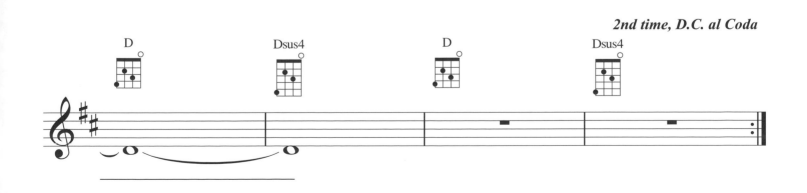

_____

Additional Lyrics

2. And I found out a long time ago
   What a woman can do to your soul.
   Ah, but she can't take you any way
   You don't already know how to go.
   And I got a... *(To Chorus)*

3. I get this feeling I may know you
   As a lover and a friend.
   But this voice keeps whispering in my other ear;
   Tells me I may never see you again.
   'Cause I get a... *(To Chorus)*

The Lion Sleeps Tonight

New Lyrics and Revised Music by George David Weiss, Hugo Peretti and Luigi Creatore

Wee _____

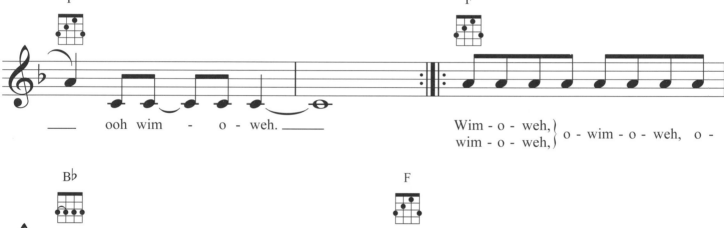

_____ ooh wim - o - weh. _____   Wim - o - weh,
                                    wim - o - weh, } o - wim - o - weh, o -

wim - o - weh, o - wim - o - weh, o - wim - o - weh, o - wim - o - weh, o -

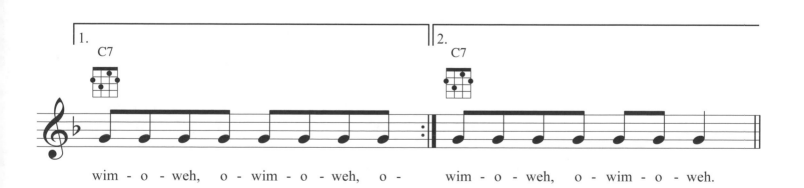

1. C7

wim - o - weh, o - wim - o - weh, o -

2. C7

wim - o - weh, o - wim - o - weh.

Puff the Magic Dragon

Words and Music by Lenny Lipton and Peter Yarrow

First note

Verse
Brightly

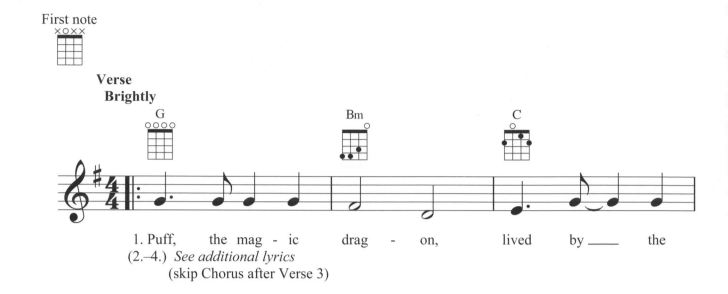

1. Puff, the mag - ic drag - on, lived by _____ the
(2.–4.) *See additional lyrics*
(skip Chorus after Verse 3)

sea and frol - icked in _____ the au - tumn mist _____ in a

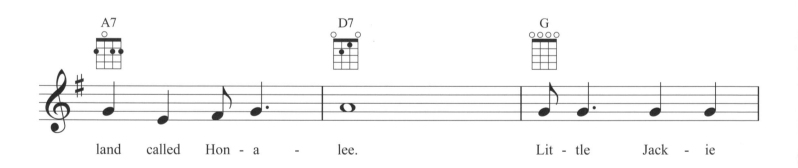

land called Hon - a - lee. Lit - tle Jack - ie

Pa - per loved that ras - cal Puff, and

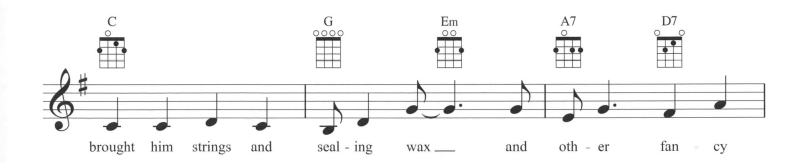

brought him strings and seal - ing wax ___ and oth - er fan - cy

Chorus

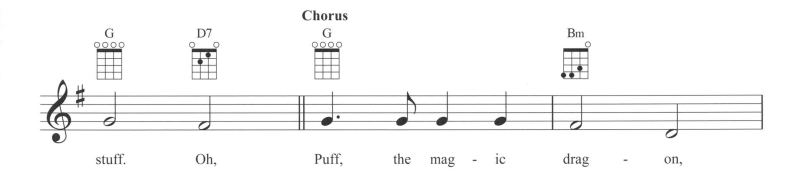

stuff. Oh, Puff, the mag - ic drag - on,

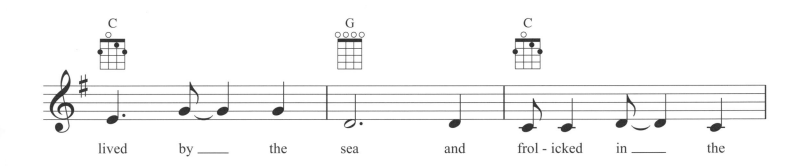

lived by ___ the sea and frol - icked in ___ the

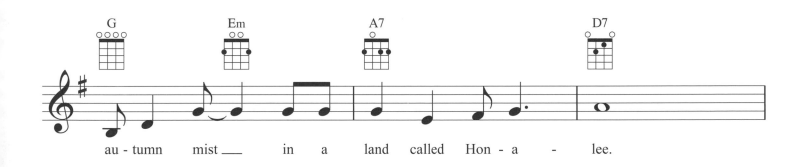

au - tumn mist ___ in a land called Hon - a - lee.

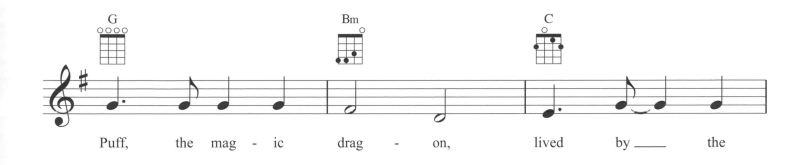

Puff, the mag - ic drag - on, lived by ___ the

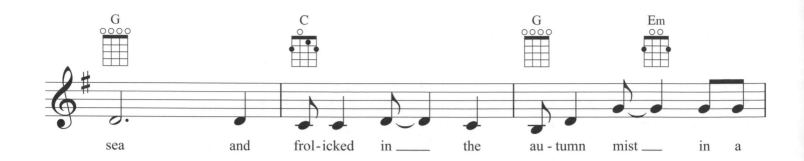

sea   and   frol-icked   in ____   the   au-tumn   mist ___   in   a

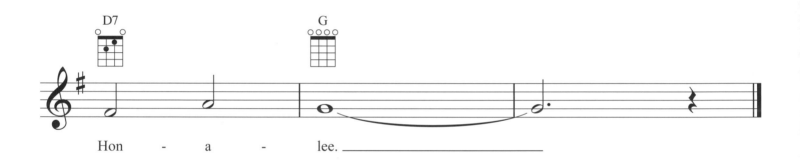

land   called   Hon - a -   lee.   2. To   land   called
                                          3. A

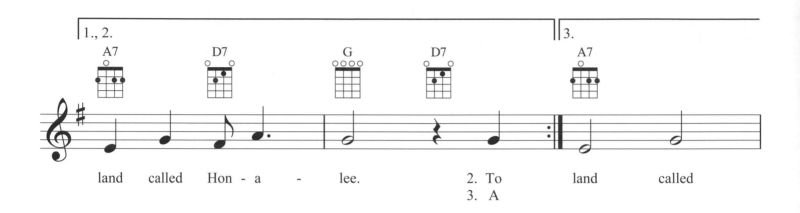

Hon - a - lee. _____

Additional Lyrics

2. Together they would travel on a boat with billowed sail,
   And Jackie kept a lookout perched on Puff's gigantic tail.
   Noble kings and princes would bow whenever they came.
   Pirate ships would lower their flags when Puff roared out his name.

3. A dragon lives forever, but not so little boys.
   Painted wings and giant rings make way for other toys.
   One gray night it happened; Jackie Paper came no more,
   And Puff, that mighty dragon, he ceased his fearless roar. *(To Verse 4)*

4. His head was bent in sorrow, green tears fell like rain.
   Puff no longer went to play along the Cherry Lane.
   Without his lifelong friend, Puff could not be brave.
   So Puff, that mighty dragon, sadly slipped into his cave.

Take Me Home, Country Roads

Words and Music by John Denver, Bill Danoff and Taffy Nivert

Sundown

Words and Music by Gordon Lightfoot

Additional Lyrics

2. She's been looking like a queen in a sailor's dream,
   And she don't always say what she really means.
   Sometimes I think it's a shame when I get feeling better when I'm feeling no pain.
   Sometimes I think it's a shame when I get feeling better when I'm feeling no pain.

3. I can picture ev'ry move that a man could make.
   Getting lost in her loving is your first mistake.
   Sundown, you better take care if I find you been creepin' 'round my back stairs.
   Sometimes I think it's a sin when I feel like I'm winning when I'm losing again.

4. I can see her looking fast in her faded jeans.
   She's a hard-loving woman, got me feeling mean.
   Sometimes I think it's a shame when I get feeling better when I'm feeling no pain.
   Sundown, you better take care if I find you been creepin' 'round my back stairs.

This Land Is Your Land

Words and Music by Woody Guthrie

Additional Lyrics

3. When the sun came shining, and I was strolling,
   And the wheat fields waving, and the dust clouds rolling,
   As the fog was lifting, a voice was chanting:
   This land was made for you and me.

4. As I went walking, I saw a sign there,
   And on the sign it said, "No Trespassing,"
   But on the other side it didn't say nothing;
   That side was made for you and me.

5. In the shadow of the steeple, I saw my people.
   By the relief office, I saw my people.
   As they stood there hungry, I stood there asking:
   Is this land made for you and me?

6. Nobody living can ever stop me
   As I go walking that freedom highway.
   Nobody living can ever make me turn back;
   This land was made for you and me.

Tie Me Kangaroo Down Sport

Words and Music by Rolf Harris

First note

Verse
Moderately, in 2

1. Watch me wal - la - by's feed, mate,
2.–6. *See additional lyrics*

watch me wal - la - by's feed. They're a dan - ger - ous

breed, mate, so watch me wal - la - by's

Chorus

feed. All to - geth - er now! Tie me kan - ga - roo

down, sport, tie me kan - ga - roo down.

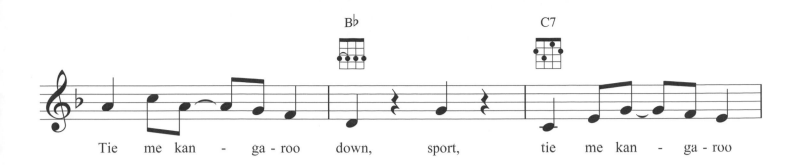

Tie me kan - ga - roo down, sport, tie me kan - ga - roo

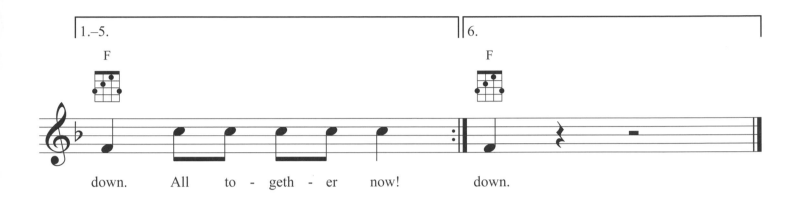

down. All to - geth - er now! down.

Additional Lyrics

2. Keep me cockatoo cool, Curl,
   Keep me cockatoo cool.
   Don't go acting the fool, Curl,
   Just keep me cockatoo cool.
   All together now!

3. Take me koala back, Jack,
   Take me koala back.
   He lives somewhere out on the track, Mac,
   So take me koala back.
   All together now!

4. Mind me platypus duck, Bill,
   Mind me platypus duck.
   Don't let him go running amok, Bill,
   Mind me platypus duck.
   All together now!

5. Play your didgeridoo, Blue,
   Play your didgeridoo.
   Keep playing 'til I shoot through, Blue.
   Play your didgeridoo.
   All together now!

6. Tan me hide when I'm dead, Fred,
   Tan me hide when I'm dead.
   So we tanned his hide when he died, Clyde,
   (Spoken:) And that's it hanging on the shed.
   All together now!

The Unicorn

Words and Music by Shel Silverstein

First note

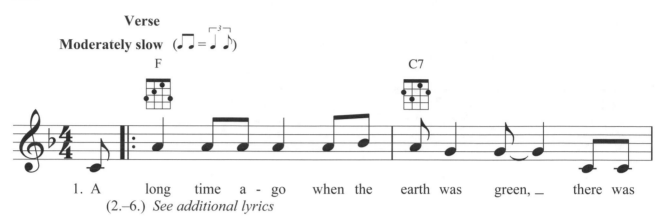

1. A long time a-go when the earth was green, _ there was
(2.–6.) *See additional lyrics*

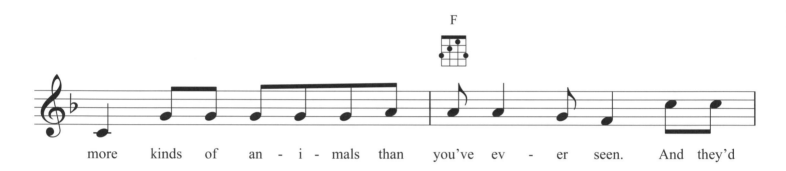

more kinds of an-i-mals than you've ev-er seen. And they'd

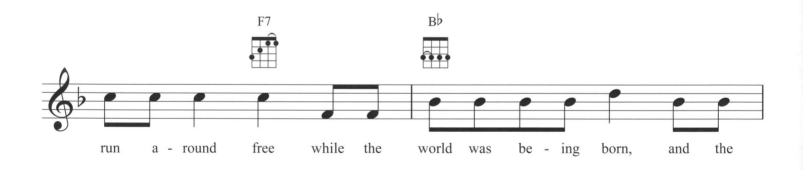

run a-round free while the world was be-ing born, and the

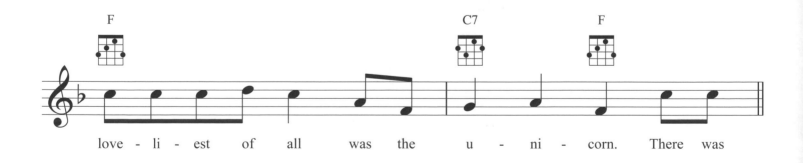

love-li-est of all was the u-ni-corn. There was

Chorus

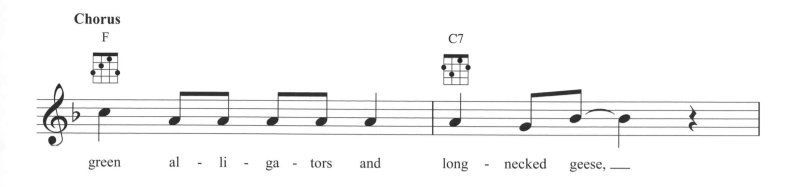

green al - li - ga - tors and long - necked geese, ___

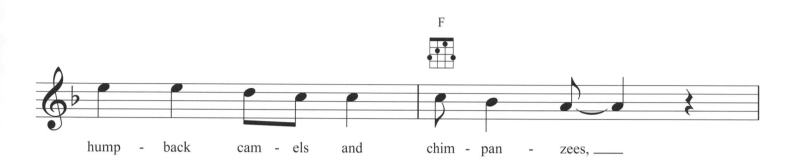

hump - back cam - els and chim - pan - zees, ___

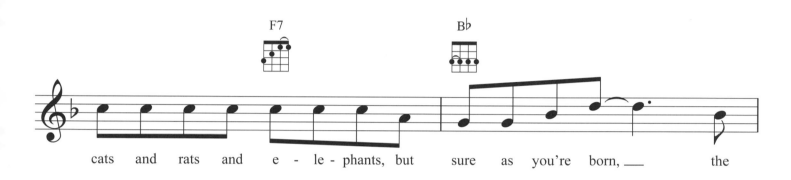

cats and rats and e - le - phants, but sure as you're born, ___ the

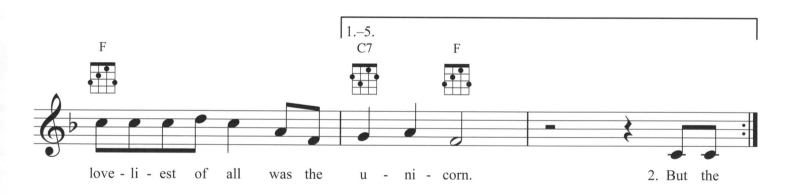

love - li - est of all was the u - ni - corn.

2. But the

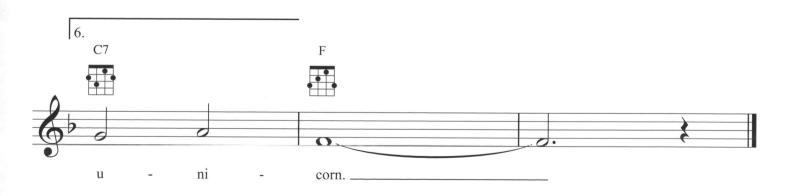

u - ni - corn. ___

Additional Lyrics

2. But the Lord seen some sinnin' and it caused him pain.
   He says, "Stand back, I'm gonna make it rain.
   So, hey, Brother Noah, I'll tell you what to do,
   Go and build me a floating zoo."
Chorus: "Two alligators and a couple of geese,
   Two hump-back camels and two chimpanzees,
   Two cats, two rats, two elephants, but sure as you're born,
   Noah, don't you forget my unicorns."

3. Now Noah was there and he answered the callin'
   And he finished up the ark as the rain started fallin'.
   Then he marched in the animals two by two,
   And he sung out as they went through:
Chorus: "Hey, Lord, I got you two alligators and a couple of geese,
   Two hump-back camels and two chimpanzees,
   Two cats, two rats, two elephants, but sure as you're born,
   Lord, I don't see your unicorns."

4. Well, Noah looked out through the drivin' rain,
   But the unicorns was hidin' — playin' silly games.
   They were kickin' and a-spashin' while the rain was pourin',
   Oh, them foolish unicorns.
Chorus: "Hey, Lord, I got you two alligators and a couple of geese,
   Two hump-back camels and two chimpanzees,
   Two cats, two rats, two elephants, but sure as you're born,
   Lord, I don't see your unicorns."

5. Then the ducks started duckin' and the snakes started snakin',
   And the elephants started elephantin' and the boat started shakin',
   The mice started squeakin' and the lions started roarin',
   And everyone's aboard but them unicorns.
Chorus: I mean the two alligators and a couple of geese,
   The hump-back camels and the chimpanzees,
   Noah cried, "Close the door 'cause the rain is pourin',
   And we just can't wait for them unicorns."

6. And then the ark started movin' and it drifted with the tide
   And the unicorns looked up from the rock and cried,
   And the water came up and sort of floated them away.
   That's why you've never seen a unicorn to this day.
Chorus: You'll see a lot of alligators and a whole mess of geese,
   You'll see hump-back camels and chimpanzees,
   You'll see cats and rats and elephants, but sure as you're born,
   You're never gonna see no unicorn.

Wagon Wheel

Words and Music by Bob Dylan and Ketch Secor

First note

Verse
Moderately fast Country

1. Head - in' down south __ to the land of the pines, __ I'm
2., 3. *See additional lyrics*

thumb - in' my way __ out of North __ Car - o - line. __

Starin' up the road __ and pray to God I __ see head -

- lights.

I

made it down the coast in sev - en - teen hours. __ Pick -

in' me a bou - quet of dog - wood flow'rs. _ And I'm a -

hop - in' for Ra - leigh, I can see my ba - by to - night. _

Chorus

So, rock _____ me, ma - ma, like a

wag - on wheel. _ Rock _____ me, ma - ma, an - y way you feel. _____ Hey, _____

ma - ma, rock _____ me.

Rock _____ me, ma - ma, like the

wind and the rain. _____ Rock _____ me, ma - ma, like a

south - bound train. Hey, _____ ma - ma, rock _

To Coda ⊕   *D.S. al Coda*

1., 2.

3.

_____ me.   Oh, _____ so rock_

⊕ **Coda**

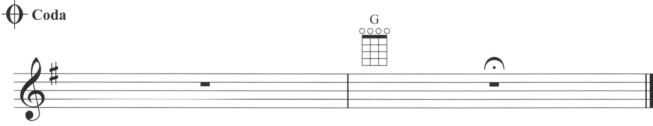

Additional Lyrics

2. Runnin' from the cold up in New England,
   I was born to be a fiddler in an old-time string band.
   My baby plays the guitar, I pick a banjo now.
   Oh, North Country winters keep a-gettin' me down.
   Lost my money playin' poker, so I had to leave town.
   But I ain't turnin' back to livin' that old life no more.

3. Walkin' through the South out of Roanoke,
   I caught a trucker out of Philly, had a nice long toke.
   But he's a-headin' west from the Cumberland Gap to Johnson City, Tennessee.
   I got, I gotta move on before the sun.
   I hear my baby callin' my name and I know that she's the only one.
   And if I die in Raleigh, at least I will die free.

You Are My Sunshine

Words and Music by Jimmie Davis

First note

Lively, in 2

Verse

1. The oth - er night, dear, _____ as I lay

(2., 3.) *See additional lyrics*

sleep - ing, _____ I dreamed I held you in my

arms. _____ When I a - woke, dear, _____ I was mis -

tak - en, _____ and I hung my

Chorus

head and cried. _____ You are my sun - shine, _____

my on - ly sun - shine, _____ you make me hap - py _____ when skies are gray. _____ You'll nev - er know, dear, _____ how much I love you. _____ Please don't take my sun - shine a -

1., 2.
way. _____ 2. I'll al - ways
3. You told me

3.
way. _____

Additional Lyrics

2. I'll always love you and make you happy
   If you will only say the same.
   But if you leave me to love another,
   You'll regret it all someday.

3. You told me once, dear, you really loved me
   And no one else could come between.
   But now you've left me and love another;
   You have shattered all my dreams.

GREAT BANJO PUBLICATIONS

FROM HAL LEONARD

Hal Leonard Banjo Method – Second Edition
by Mac Robertson, Robbie Clement, Will Schmid
This innovative method teaches 5-string banjo bluegrass style using a carefully paced approach that keeps beginners playing great songs *while learning*. Book 1 covers easy chord strums, tablature, right-hand rolls, hammer-ons, slides and pull-offs, and more. Book 2 includes solos and licks, fiddle tunes, back-up, capo use, and more.

00699500 Book 1 Book Only $7.99
00695101 Book 1 Book/Online Audio $16.99
00699502 Book 2 Book Only $7.99

Banjo Aerobics
A 50-Week Workout Program for Developing, Improving and Maintaining Banjo Technique
by Michael Bremer
Take your banjo playing to the next level with this fantastic daily resource, providing a year's worth of practice material with a two-week vacation. The accompanying audio includes demo tracks for all the examples in the book to reinforce how the banjo should sound.

00113734 Book/Online Audio $19.99

Banjo Chord Finder
This extensive reference guide covers over 2,800 banjo chords, including four of the most commonly used tunings. Thirty different chord qualities are covered for each key, and each chord quality is presented in two different voicings. Also includes a lesson on chord construction and a fingerboard chart of the banjo neck!

00695741 9 x 12................... $8.99 00695742 6 x 9..................... $6.99

Banjo Scale Finder
by Chad Johnson
Learn to play scales on the banjo with this comprehensive yet easy-to-use book. It contains more than 1,300 scale diagrams for the most often-used scales and modes, including multiple patterns for each scale. Also includes a lesson on scale construction and a fingerboard chart of the banjo neck.

00695780 9 x 12................... $9.99 00695783 6 x 9..................... $6.99

First 50 Songs You Should Play on Banjo
arr. Michael J. Miles & Greg Cahill
Easy-to-read banjo tab, chord symbols and lyrics for the most popular songs banjo players like to play. Explore clawhammer and three-finger-style banjo in a variety of tunings and capoings with this one-of-a-kind collection. Songs include: Angel from Montgomery • Carolina in My Mind • Cripple Creek • Danny Boy • The House of the Rising Sun • Mr. Tambourine Man • Take Me Home, Country Roads • This Land Is Your Land • Wildwood Flower • and many more.

00153311 ....$14.99

Fretboard Roadmaps
by Fred Sokolow
This handy book/with online audio will get you playing all over the banjo fretboard in any key! You'll learn to: increase your chord, scale and lick vocabulary • play chord-based licks, moveable major and blues scales, melodic scales and first-position major scales • and much more! The audio includes 51 demonstrations of the exercises.

00695358 Book/Online Audio $15.99

O Brother, Where Art Thou?
Banjo tab arrangements of 12 bluegrass/folk songs from this Grammy-winning album. Includes: The Big Rock Candy Mountain • Down to the River to Pray • I Am a Man of Constant Sorrow • I Am Weary (Let Me Rest) • I'll Fly Away • In the Jailhouse Now • Keep on the Sunny Side • You Are My Sunshine • and more, plus lyrics and a banjo notation legend.

00699528 Banjo Tablature... $14.99

Earl Scruggs and the 5-String Banjo
Earl Scruggs' legendary method has helped thousands of banjo players get their start. It features everything you need to know to start playing, even how to build your own banjo! Topics covered include: Scruggs tuners • how to read music • chords • how to read tablature • anatomy of Scruggs-style picking • exercises in picking • 44 songs • biographical notes • and more! The online audio features Earl Scruggs playing and explaining over 60 examples!

00695764 Book Only.. $24.99
00695765 Book/Online Audio.. $34.99

Clawhammer Cookbook
Tools, Techniques & Recipes for Playing Clawhammer Banjo
by Michael Bremer
The goal of this book isn't to tell you how to play tunes or how to play like anyone else. It's to teach you ways to approach, arrange, and personalize any tune – to develop your own unique style. To that end, we'll take in a healthy serving of old-time music and also expand the clawhammer palate to taste a few other musical styles. Includes audio track demos of all the songs and examples to aid in the learning process.

00118354 Book/Online Audio.......................................$19.99

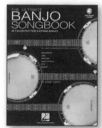

The Ultimate Banjo Songbook
A great collection of banjo classics: Alabama Jubilee • Bye Bye Love • Duelin' Banjos • The Entertainer • Foggy Mountain Breakdown • Great Balls of Fire • Lady of Spain • Orange Blossom Special • (Ghost) Riders in the Sky • Rocky Top • San Antonio Rose • Tennessee Waltz • UFO-TOFU • You Are My Sunshine • and more.

00699565 Book/Online Audio.. $27.50